DOWNSIDE
OF DRUGS

New Drugs

Bath Salts, Spice, Salvia, & Designer Drugs

DOWNSIDE OF DRUGS

ADHD Medication Abuse: Ritalin®, Adderall®, & Other Addictive Stimulants

Alcohol & Tobacco

Caffeine: Energy Drinks, Coffee, Soda, & Pills

Dangerous Depressants & Sedatives

Doping: Human Growth Hormone, Steroids, & Other Performance-Enhancing Drugs

Hard Drugs: Cocaine, LSD, PCP, & Heroin

Marijuana: Legal & Developmental Consequences

Methamphetamine & Other Amphetamines

New Drugs: Bath Salts, Spice, Salvia, & Designer Drugs

Over-the-Counter Medications

Prescription Painkillers: OxyContin®, Percocet®, Vicodin®, & Other Addictive Analgesics

DOWNSIDE OF DRUGS

New Drugs
Bath Salts, Spice, Salvia, & Designer Drugs

Celicia Scott

Mason Crest

Mason Crest
450 Parkway Drive, Suite D
Broomall, PA 19008
www.masoncrest.com

Printed and bound in the United States of America.

9 8 7 6 5 4 3 2

Series ISBN: 978-1-4222-3015-2
Hardcover ISBN: 978-1-4222-3024-4
Paperback ISBN: 978-1-4222-3193-7
ebook ISBN: 978-1-4222-8810-8

Cataloging-in-Publication Data on file with the Library of Congress.

Contents

INTRODUCTION

One of the best parts of getting older is the opportunity to make your own choices. As your parents give you more space and you spend more time with friends than family, you are called upon to make more decisions for yourself. Many important decisions that present themselves in the teen years may change your life. The people with whom you are friendly, how much effort you put into school and other activities, and what kinds of experiences you choose for yourself all affect the person you will become as you emerge from being a child into becoming a young adult.

One of the most important decisions you will make is whether or not you use substances like alcohol, marijuana, crystal meth, and cocaine. Even using prescription medicines incorrectly or relying on caffeine to get through your daily life can shape your life today and your future tomorrow. These decisions can impact all the other decisions you make. If you decide to say yes to drug abuse, the impact on your life is usually not a good one!

One suggestion I make to many of my patients is this: think about how you will respond to an offer to use drugs before it happens. In the heat of the moment, particularly if you're feeling some peer pressure, it can be hard to think clearly—so be prepared ahead of time. Thinking about why you don't want to use drugs and how you'll respond if you are asked to use them can make it easier to make a healthy decision when the time comes. Just like practicing a sport makes it easier to play in a big game, having thought about why drugs aren't a good fit for you and exactly what you might say to avoid them can give you the "practice" you need to do what's best for you. It can make a tough situation simpler once it arises.

In addition, talk about drugs with your parents or a trusted adult. This will both give you support and help you clarify your thinking. The decision is still yours to make, but adults can be a good resource. Take advantage of the information and help they can offer you.

Sometimes, young people fall into abusing drugs without really thinking about it ahead of time. It can sometimes be hard to recognize when you're making a decision that might hurt you. You might be with a friend or acquaintance in a situation that feels comfortable. There may be things in your life that are hard, and it could seem like using drugs might make them easier. It's also natural to be curious about new experiences. However, by not making a decision ahead of time, you may be actually making a decision without realizing it, one that will limit your choices in the future.

When someone offers you drugs, there is no flashing sign that says, "Hey, think about what you're doing!" Making a good decision may be harder because the "fun" part happens immediately while the downside—the damage to your brain and the rest of your body—may not be obvious right away. One of the biggest downsides of drugs is that they have long-term effects on your life. They could reduce your educational, career, and relationship opportunities. Drug use often leaves users with more problems than when they started.

Whenever you make a decision, it's important to know all the facts. When it comes to drugs, you'll need answers to questions like these: How do different drugs work? Is there any "safe" way to use drugs? How will drugs hurt my body and my brain? If I don't notice any bad effects right away, does that mean these drugs are safe? Are these drugs addictive? What are the legal consequences of using drugs? This book discusses these questions and helps give you the facts to make good decisions.

Reading this book is a great way to start, but if you still have questions, keep looking for the answers. There is a lot of information on the Internet, but not all of it is reliable. At the back of this book, you'll find a list of more books and good websites for finding out more about this drug. A good website is teens.drugabuse.gov, a site compiled for teens by the National Institute on Drug Abuse (NIDA). This is a reputable federal government agency that researches substance use and how to prevent it. This website does a good job looking at a lot of data and consolidating it into easy-to-understand messages.

What if you are worried you already have a problem with drugs? If that's the case, the best thing to do is talk to your doctor or another trusted adult to help figure out what to do next. They can help you find a place to get treatment.

Drugs have a downside—but as a young adult, you have the power to make decisions for yourself about what's best for you. Use your power wisely!

—*Joshua Borus, MD*

1. WHAT ARE SOME OF THE NEW DRUGS ON THE STREET?

There are new drugs out there these days. They're spreading fast because people often get them on the Internet. Sometimes they're called "designer drugs," because they've been specially designed to create certain effects in their users. They may be like older drugs in some ways, but their chemicals have been *modified* in some way. People have worked on them to make them stronger or to try to get rid of side effects. These new drugs are different from the old ones. Some of them are even legal, so kids think they must be safe.

A lot of these drugs have psychedelic properties. This means they change the way your brain perceives things. Everything may seem brighter and more intense. Life may seem more meaningful.

But these drugs have a big downside.

Bath salts are one of the new designer drugs. They're white crystals that look like real bath salts, the kind you put in your bathwater, but they're not really the same thing at all. Sometimes, though, they're sold in bath-salt packaging, to disguise what they really are.

Another new drug is sometimes called "spice" and sometimes "K2." It's really a form of *synthetic* marijuana. It's made by spraying natural herbs with synthetic chemicals. It's often sold and packaged as "herbal incense" or "herbal smoking blends."

Unlike many of the other new drugs, salvia is a plant that's been around for thousands of years. People sometimes grow it in their garden because it has pretty flowers. It's not really new—but it's new as a street drug. When it's smoked or chewed, it can make people *hallucinate*.

There are literally hundreds of other new designer drugs. They have names like Ket and Jib, Tweeker and Max, Eve and Death. People smoke them in cigars and cigarettes. They take them in tablet forms and in capsules. They shoot them up in needles. They mix them together. Many times people don't even know for sure what they're taking.

2. WHAT ARE THE DOWNSIDES OF THESE DRUGS?

Because most of these drugs are new on the street, *researchers* haven't had many chances to study them. Scientists aren't really sure how all of these drugs affect humans. But they do know that many of these drugs are dangerous.

A designer drug called Bromo-Dragon-Fly—or simply FLY—makes blood vessels become so narrow that blood can't flow to the hands and feet. Its effects are a little like leprosy, a disease where people can lose their toes and fingers. In 2007, a man who took FLY ended up losing several fingers and the front parts of both his feet. In 2009, another man who took FLY died. His friend who was tripping with him survived, but he said that taking FLY was "like being dragged to hell and back again. Many times. It is the most evil thing I've ever tried. It lasted an eternity."

In 2011, two young adults thought they were taking another designer drug called 2C-E; they took the normal dose for 2C-E, but they were actually taking FLY, so the dose they took was about 100 times the correct dose. Both kids vomited blood. They had terrifying hallucinations. And then they died.

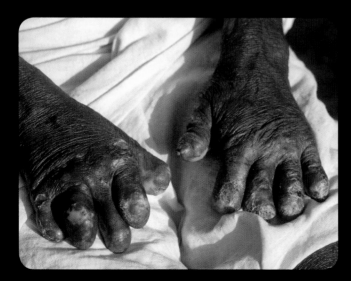

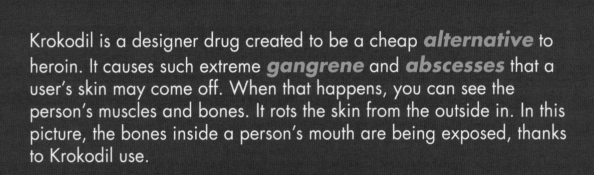

Krokodil is a designer drug created to be a cheap **alternative** to heroin. It causes such extreme **gangrene** and **abscesses** that a user's skin may come off. When that happens, you can see the person's muscles and bones. It rots the skin from the outside in. In this picture, the bones inside a person's mouth are being exposed, thanks to Krokodil use.

PMA—a drug that also goes by the name Dr. Death, Chicken Yellow, and Pink Ecstasy—causes nausea, vomiting, and hallucinations. Its effects are **unpredictable**, though. Some people are more **sensitive** to it than others. It also takes a while to take effect, so sometimes people take a dose—and then take another one because they think the first one didn't work. Then they end up dead.

3. WHAT ARE THE LEGAL CONSEQUENCES OF USING THESE NEW DRUGS FOR YOUNG PEOPLE?

Because many of these drugs are so new, laws haven't always been passed yet to ban or *regulate* their use. In the United States, a law was passed that made it illegal to make, sell, or possess chemicals that are a lot like other drugs that are already illegal. But designer drugs are often specifically designed to get around legal regulation. They are made from chemical compounds that are not currently illegal but that *mimic* the effects of other more commonly known drugs (which are illegal).

If you're caught driving while under the influence of one of the new drugs, it's against the law (even if the drug itself isn't illegal). Driving while ability *impaired* (DWAI) is illegal in most states in the United States. If you're high, you shouldn't be driving!

In Canada and parts of Europe, the new drugs are being banned as officials become aware of them.

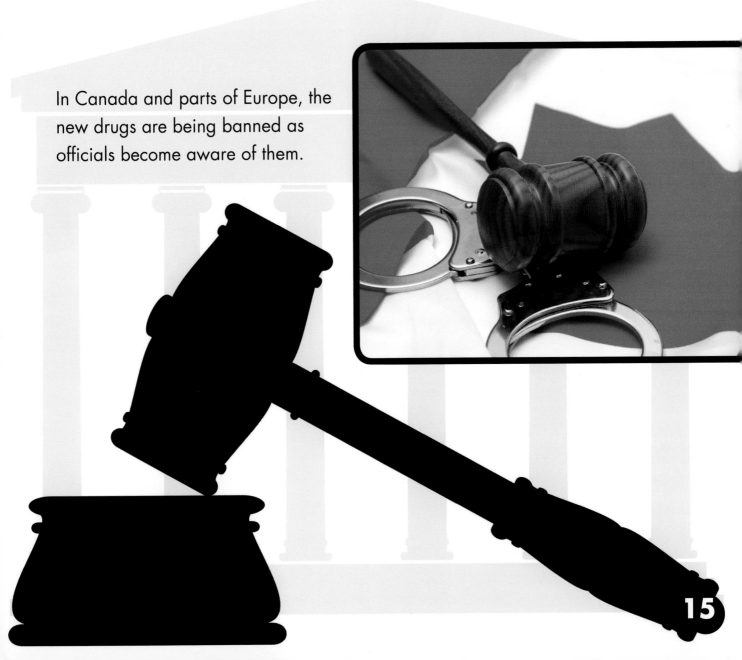

4. WHAT HAPPENS TO YOUR BODY WHEN YOU USE BATH SALTS?

Drugs are any chemicals that change the way your body works. Drugs can do good things—like cure diseases and ease pain. They can also be very dangerous. Bath salts are powerful drugs.

People taking bath salts may not notice pain as much. This may seem like a good thing—but pain also protects us from injuries. If you can't tell that you're being burned, for example, you could end up with a serious injury.

People who use bath salts often get a headache. Their hearts start to flutter and beat irregularly. They may feel sick to their stomach or throw up. They get *dehydrated*.

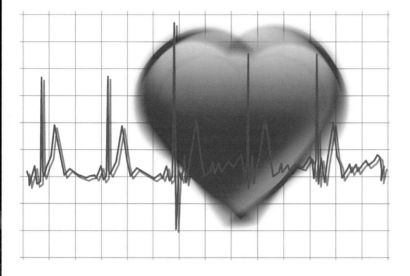

Bath salts are a type of drug called a stimulant. Stimulants speed up your body's processes and reactions. Bath salts work a lot like amphetamines and cocaine. They make your heart beat faster.

People taking bath salts feel revved up. Their blood pressure goes higher. They may feel twitchy.

Too much bath salts can be deadly. They can cause heart attacks, kidney failure, and liver failure. The tissues of your muscles can start to break down.

5. WHAT HAPPENS TO YOUR BODY WHEN YOU USE SPICE?

Because spice is fairly new, scientists and doctors haven't had a chance yet to study it carefully. They're not sure about all the effects that it can have on your body. However, some people who have taken spice have had heart attacks. Others have had *convulsions*.

When it comes to spice, you really don't know exactly what is in the mix. Many different ingredients have been found in it that could harm your body in various ways. People who are taken to emergency rooms after using spice have symptoms that include rapid heart rate, vomiting, *agitation*, confusion, and hallucinations. The drug has also been linked to acute kidney injuries, which left untreated, can cause the kidneys to shut down.

The scientist who first created many of the chemicals used in spice, Professor John W. Huffman, said, "People who use it are idiots."

THE EFFECTS ON YOUR BODY WHEN YOU USE SPICE

Psychosis

Glazed expression, red eyes

Inability to speak

Body temperature fluctuation, inability to feel pain, seizures

Increase blood pressure and heartrate, heart attack

Temporary paralysis, cramping

Kidney failure, vomiting

6. WHAT HAPPENS TO YOUR BODY WHEN YOU USE SALVIA?

When people are using salvia, they may become clumsy and dizzy. Their speech may be slurred. Their vision is impaired. Because of these symptoms, using salvia while driving or using machinery is very dangerous.

Effects of
Salvia divinorum

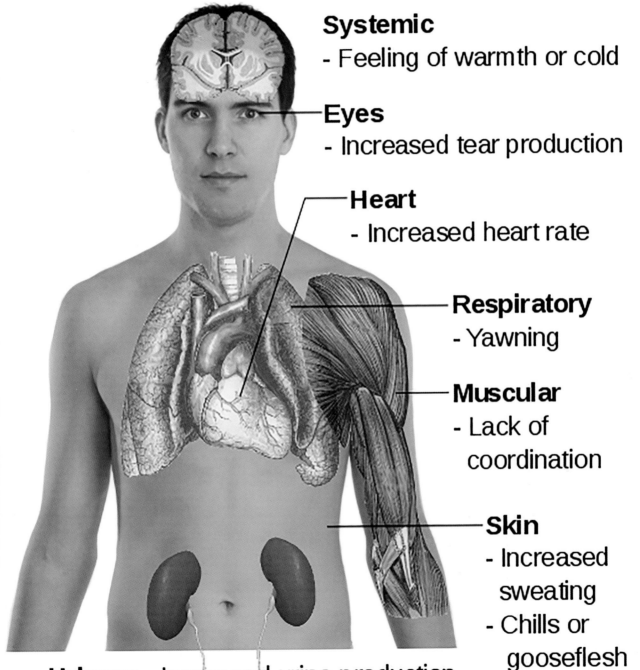

Systemic
- Feeling of warmth or cold

Eyes
- Increased tear production

Heart
- Increased heart rate

Respiratory
- Yawning

Muscular
- Lack of coordination

Skin
- Increased sweating
- Chills or gooseflesh

Urinary - Increased urine production

7. WHAT HAPPENS TO YOUR BODY WHEN YOU USE SOME OF THE OTHER NEW DRUGS?

Different types of designer drugs do different things to your body. Some of these drugs will keep you from sleeping and take away your appetite. They may make you very relaxed. Some designer drugs cause people to have increased heart rates (which could lead to heart attacks), sweating, chills, slurred speech, nausea, tremors, as well as symptoms that look like a disease called Parkinson's where your muscles *spasm* and move *involuntarily*. Some of these drugs can make you lose consciousness.

Since many of these drugs are made in labs that are illegal or dishonest, the drugs' ingredients may vary a lot. Some batches may be very strong, while others will be quite weak. Because of this, it's hard for users to know what's "safe" to take. A dose that causes very little effects one time might make someone very sick or even kill her the next time.

The dangers of some drugs are very well understood. Drugs like marijuana, heroin, and cocaine have been around for many years, so scientists have studied them for a long time. These are still very dangerous substances, but at least doctors know how to treat *overdoses* of these drugs. Because scientists and doctors are still learning about these newer drugs, however, they're still learning how to treat people who abuse them. This makes using these drugs even more dangerous.

DANGER

8. HOW DO BATH SALTS CHANGE YOUR BRAIN?

The manmade chemicals in bath salts include mephedrone (known on the street sometimes as "Drone," "Meph," or "Meow Meow") and methylone, but there are many other chemicals as well. There's a lot scientists still don't know about how these chemicals will change your brain. They do know that these chemicals act a lot like amphetamines. They also act like another designer drug, MDMA (usually known on the street as "Ecstasy").

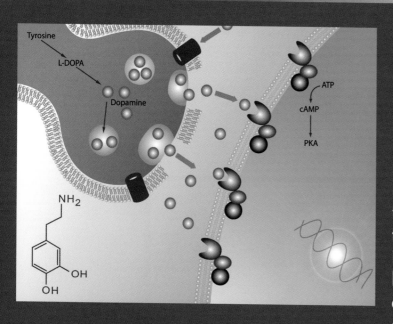

Drugs like these make human brains produce more of a chemical called dopamine. Dopamine is a neurotransmitter. That means its job in the brain is to carry messages between nerve cells. Dopamine is one of the main neurotransmitters that make people feel good when they do something they enjoy. A rush of dopamine inside your brain makes you feel happy and full of energy. That's a good thing—except that drugs can give you shots of dopamine that are too much for your brain and body to handle. Your brain sends out messages to the rest of your body that can raise your heart rate and blood pressure to dangerous levels.

A recent study found that one of the most common chemicals in bath salts raises brain dopamine the same way cocaine does—but the chemical in bath salts was at least 10 times stronger than cocaine.

Some of the other chemicals in bath salts are a lot like the chemicals in LSD. These chemicals do other things to your brain. They make you hallucinate. In other words, if you use bath salts, you might see and hear things that aren't really there. Some of these things can be very scary. They can make you do things you would never normally do.

In 2012, a thirty-one-year-old man got high on bath salts. Then he stripped off his clothes—and attacked an old homeless man. When police found the naked man on a major road in Miami, he was chewing on the homeless man's face. Before police could stop him, the naked man had ripped off most of the other man's face and gouged out his eyes. The homeless man survived the incident. The naked man didn't. The police shot and killed him.

Spice is another fairly new drug, so researchers haven't had a chance yet to study what it does to the brain. They do know, though, that the chemicals found in spice attach to the same nerve cells as THC, the main mind-altering chemical in marijuana. Some of the chemicals found in spice, however, attach to these cells more strongly, which leads to a much stronger and more unpredictable effect.

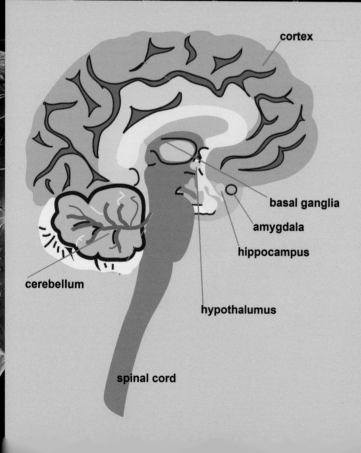

cortex

basal ganglia

amygdala

hippocampus

hypothalamus

cerebellum

spinal cord

These chemicals change the brain's normal reactions by interfering with the processes in a whole bunch of brain structures. They change the amygdala, which regulates fear and anxiety—so the user may feel panicky and scared. They change the basal ganglia, which regulates our decisions to move in response to something—so the user's reaction time will be slowed. They change the hippocampus, which is where we learn new information—so the user's memory won't be as good. They change the cortex, where we do our most complicated thinking—so the user's judgment will be altered.

Many spice users have experiences similar to what they would experience if they used marijuana. They feel very relaxed. Their brains' **perceptions** change. In some cases, the effects are stronger than those caused by marijuana. Some users report feeling extremely anxious. They may feel frightened and **paranoid**. They may have hallucinations.

Some varieties of spice also contain substances that could cause very different effects than the user might be expecting. These could be stronger and more dangerous than anything the user is prepared for.

10. HOW DOES SALVIA CHANGE YOUR BRAIN?

Salvia's effects on the brain don't last very long—but while they last, they're powerful. People who abuse it generally experience hallucinations. They may completely lose contact with reality. For some people, this can be a lot like a *psychotic episode*. In other words, it's a lot like being crazy! In this state of mind, people may also feel anxious and scared. They may lose their memories of everything that happens during the episode.

After using salvia, once the "high" is over, users sometimes have a feeling of intense emotional discomfort or uneasiness.

Salvia is a hallucinogen—it makes your brain perceive strange things that aren't real. Hallucinogens like salvia are always risky because they upset your brain's normal functions. When you're hallucinating, your brain loses its normal abilities to protect you from danger.

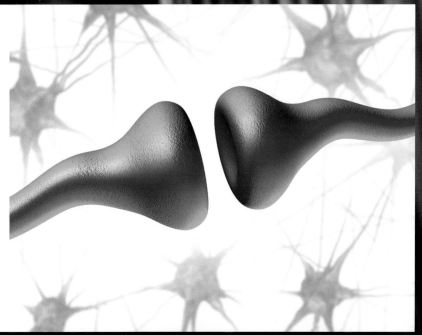

Salvia contains a chemical called *salvinorin A*. It changes the way your brain cells work by attaching to what are called opioid **receptors**. These receptors play a role in how our bodies perceive pain. They also help to keep our brains balanced and sane.

The chemical effects of salvia may make your brain see the world in a strange, **distorted** way. Colors may seem brighter. You may feel as though you're floating in another reality, separated from the world around you. These feelings can be very intense. They may not feel very nice.

11. HOW DO SOME OF THE OTHER NEW DRUGS CHANGE YOUR BRAIN?

Drugs tap into the brain's communication system. They change the way nerve cells normally send, receive, and process information. Different drugs—because of their chemical structures—work differently. Some drugs can change the brain in ways that last long after the person has stopped taking drugs. This is more likely when someone takes a drug over and over for a long period of time.

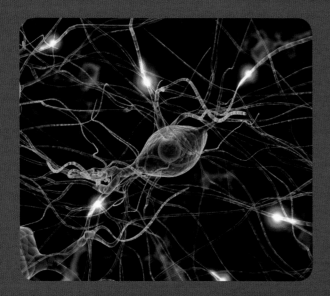

Some drugs *activate* nerve cells because the drug's chemical structure mimics that of one of the brain's natural neurotransmitters. The drugs "fool" the brain cells' receptors. They don't work the same way as a natural neurotransmitter, though, so the nerve cells send abnormal messages through the brain and to the rest of your body. Other drugs make nerve cells release the brain's natural neurotransmitters in huge quantities. This makes the brain send out messages to the body that are exaggerated or too "loud."

"Ecstasy" and "Molly" are slang terms for a designer drug called MDMA, which is short for 3,4-methylenedioxymethamphetamine. Researchers think that MDMA may affect nerve cells that use a brain chemical called serotonin to communicate with other nerve cells. Serotonin plays a direct role in controlling mood, aggression, sexual activity, sleep, and sensitivity to pain. Scientists have also seen memory loss in people who use MDMA regularly. A study of animals showed that exposure to high doses of MDMA for just four days caused brain damage that could still be seen six to seven years later.

Ketamine (sometimes called Special K or just K) is yet another designer drug. Scientists first developed it be used as anesthesia during surgery, but now it's often used as a street drug. It causes changes in the brain that start out with a "rush." Music may seem louder, but ketamine shuts off the brain's ability to hear certain kinds of other sounds, and it "turns down" the brain's ability to taste and smell. The changes inside the brain make the person feel removed from his own body. He may not be able to see or hear others. He may experience something that seems a lot like a near-death experience.

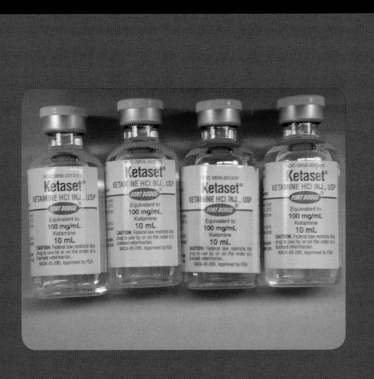

12. ARE THESE NEW DRUGS ADDICTIVE?

When a person is addicted to something, she cannot control how often she uses it. She depends on it to help her cope with daily life. Her body needs it in order to function. If she tries to quit using it, she goes through withdrawal. Her body now needs the chemical in order to function, and without it, she feels sick.

Because many of these new drugs are chemically so much like other addictive drugs, it's safe to assume that most of them are also addictive.

Bath salts are chemically a lot like cocaine, meth, and ampheramines, all of which are very addictive. Frequent use causes dependence and severe withdrawal symptoms.

Spice also appears to very addictive. In experiments done on rats, if the rats could get as much of the chemical as they wanted, they helped themselves to it more and more.

13. WHO USES BATH SALTS?

More and more young people are using bath salts to get high. More males than females abuse bath salts. They tend to be younger than the users of other drugs.

The number of people abusing bath salts has increased rapidly. In 2010, poison-control centers in the United States only received 302 calls related to bath salts. That number increased to 1,782 calls in just the first four months of 2011, and by October of that year, it had gone up to more than 5,000 calls. At first, most of the calls to poison-control centers came from Louisiana, Florida, and Kentucky, but later, bath salts abuse had expanded to 33 states in the United States.

Invigorating Bath Salt

250 mg

As of 2011, bath salts were the sixth most commonly used drug (after tobacco, alcohol, marijuana, cocaine, and Ecstasy). They may come in pretty packages like this one—but they're still a dangerous drug!

Most people who use bath salts use it at least weekly—and most of them snort or inhale the drug in some other way. This causes a more intense high—and a higher risk of addiction and complications.

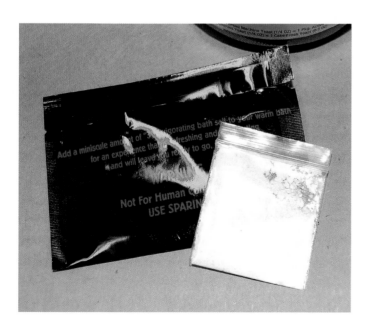

Some of the many street or slang names for bath salts:

- Red Dove
- Purple Wave
- Blue Silk
- Ivory Wave
- Vanilla Sky
- Bliss
- Magic
- White Lightning
- White Dove
- Super Coke
- Tranquility
- Zoom

Spice is popular among young people. It's the second most popular drug among high-school seniors (after marijuana). Teenagers often think it's safe, "natural," and legal, which has helped make it so popular.

HERE'S WHAT THE U.S. NAVY HAS TO SAY ABOUT SPICE.

15. WHO USES SALVIA?

Salvia abuse has increased in young adults between eighteen and twenty-five. Males abuse salvia more than females. However, although many young adults have tried salvia, not that many use it regularly.

In the most recent study on young people using salvia, the 2006 National Survey on Drug Use and Health, about 1.8 million young adults over age twelve said they had used salvia at some point in their life.

Salvia was never meant to be a party drug. *Salvia divinorum* was originally used by the native people of Oaxaca, Mexico, as part of their spritual ceremonies, and it is still used for that purpose in Mexico today. The people believe the plant is a form of the Virgin Mary who comes to help them see religious visions. When they use salvia, they go to a quiet place, where they began their ceremonies with prayers to Mary, the Holy Trinity, and the saints. Their priests say that salvia, "speaks with a quiet voice" during times of deep meditation.

16. MORE QUESTIONS?

What should I do if I think someone has overdosed on one of these new drugs?

An overdose is when someone takes too much of any drug or medication, so that it causes serious, harmful symptoms or even death. If you think you or someone else has overdosed on a drug, you should always call 911 immediately. If it's not an emergency but you have questions about preventing an overdose, you can also call the National Poison Control Center (1-800-222-1222) from anywhere in the United States. It is a free call and it's *confidential*. You can call for any reason, 24/7.

Can I use designer drugs and stay safe?

The only way to stay completely safe is not to use any of these drugs. Remember, it's hard to know the strength of these drugs or if they've had other chemicals added to them, which makes their use even more dangerous. The following practices make them even MORE risky:

- Mixing drugs, including alcohol, with any of these drugs increases the risk of overdose or death.
- Boosting (taking more of these drugs while already high) is even riskier.
- Taking these drugs alone or with people who might take advantage of you could put you in a dangerous situation. These drugs can affect your ability to recognize danger or make smart decisions.
- Driving a vehicle while using any of these drugs could kill you—or someone else.

FURTHER READING

Abadinsky, Howard. *Drug Use and Abuse.* Stamford, Conn.: Cengage, 2013.

Adams, Taite. *Who Is Molly? Molly Drug Facts, What is Ecstasy, and Life-Saving MDMA Effects Info.* New York: Rapid Response, 2013.

Carlson, Dale. *Addiction: The Brain Disease.* Branford, Conn.: Bick, 2010.

Emmett, David. *Understanding Street Drugs.* London, UK: Jessica Kingsley, 2005.

Olive, M. Foster. *Designer Drugs.* New York: Chelsea House, 2004.

Parks, Peggy. *Bath Salts and Other Synthetic Drugs.* San Diego, Calif.: Referencepoint, 2013.

Shelton, C. D. *Addiction: Understanding Addiction.* Harrison, Va.: Choice, 2013.

FIND OUT MORE ONLINE

Bath Salts: Poison Control
www.aapcc.org/alerts/bath-salts

Bath Salts Drug Trend
www.webmd.com/mental-health/features/bath-salts-drug-dangers

Designer Drugs
www.livestrong.com/article/227581-what-are-the-different-types-of-designer-drugs

Drug Facts: MDMA (Ecstasy or Molly)
www.drugabuse.gov/publications/drugfacts/mdma-ecstasy-or-molly

Drug Facts: Salvia
www.drugabuse.gov/publications/drugfacts/salvia

Drug Facts: Spice
www.drugabuse.gov/publications/drugfacts/spice-synthetic-marijuana

Popular Science: Synthetic Marijuana
www.popsci.com/science/article/2013-04/synthetic-marijuana-what-is-it

The Straight Dope on What Bath Salts Do to Your Brain
www.forbes.com/sites/daviddisalvo/2012/06/05/the-straight-dope-on-what-bath-salts-do-to-your-brain-and-why-theyre-dangerous

GLOSSARY

abscesses: Swollen parts of your body, filled with pus.

activate: Switch on; make something work.

agitation: A state of anxiety or nervous excitement.

alternative: Another option.

confidential: Kept a secret.

convulsions: Powerful muscle spasms that you can't control.

dehydrated: When your body doesn't have enough water to function properly.

distorted: Warped or twisted.

gangrene: When a part of your body dies and begins to decompose.

hallucinate: See or hear things that aren't really there.

impaired: Having your abilities damaged in some way.

involuntarily: Outside of your control.

mimic: Imitate or copy.

modified: Changed or altered.

overdoses: When someone takes too much of a drug, resulting in the drug being toxic.

paranoid: Being anxious, suspicious, or distrustful without having a good reason.

perceptions: Things you see, hear, smell, taste, and feel.

psychotic episode: A period of time where you lose contact with reality and act as if you are insane.

receptors: The parts of your cells that attach to chemicals like neurotransmitters and hormones.

regulate: Control or place limits on.

researchers: Scientists who try to make new discoveries.

sensitive: How much your body responds to a drug.

spasm: A sudden, involuntary muscle contraction.

synthetic: Artificially created.

unpredictable: Impossible to know the result.

INDEX

PICTURE CREDITS

pp. 10–11
Schorle
DEA
Dreamstime:
Michele Loftus
Elena Schweitzer
John Bigl

pp. 12–13
B. Jehle
Psychonaught
Demiurge
Dreamstime:
Mark Payne
Uludag Sozluk

pp. 14–15
Dreamstime:
Alexander Sobolev
John Takai
Matthew Benoit

pp. 16–17
Dreamstime:
Cornelius20
Ariwasabi
Czuber
Sergey Eshemtove
LuckyNick
Stock Illusrations Ltd.
London England

pp. 18–19
Maximus Foundation
Dreamstime:
Slobodan Mračina
Shubhangi Kene

pp. 20–21
Maximus Foundation
Dreamstime:
Albachiaraa
Shubhangi Kene

pp. 22–23
Dreamstime:
Shubhangi Kene
Arsgara

pp. 24–25
DEA
Dreamstime:
Alphaspirit
Meletios Verras
Marek Redesiuk
Haywire Media

pp. 26–27
Vestal Creative Service
Dreamstime:
Alex Fiodorov
Mad Artists
Shubhangi Kene

pp. 28–29
Dreamstime:
Rolff Images
Paul Fleet
SkyPixel
Dimjul
Christophe Testi

pp. 30–31
Schlonz
Navmans
Dreamstime:
Andreus
Sebastian Kaulitzki

pp. 32–33
Dreamstime:
Margaret M. Stewart
Yeyen Design
Vladimir Lukovic

pp. 34–35
New York State Senate
DEA
Dreamstime:
Flavijus

pp. 36–37
New Zealand Government
US Navy

pp. 38–39
Dreamstime:
Shining Colors
Julio Aldana
Kristy Pargeter

pp. 40–41
Dreamstime:
Shubhangi Kene

ABOUT THE AUTHOR
AND THE CONSULTANT

CELICIA SCOTT lives in New York State. She worked in teaching before starting a second career as a writer.

DR. JOSHUA BORUS, MD, MPH, graduated from the Harvard Medical School and the Harvard School of Public Health. He completed a residency in pediatrics and then served as chief resident at Floating Hospital for Children at Tufts Medical Center before completing a fellowship in Adolescent Medicine at Boston Children's Hospital. He is currently an attending physician in the Division of Adolescent and Young Adult Medicine at Boston Children's Hospital and an instructor of pediatrics at Harvard Medical School.